Leading Others, Managing Yourself

Your board, staff, or clients may also benefit from this book's insight. For more information on quantity discounts, contact the Health Administration Press Marketing Manager at (312) 424-9470.

Library of Congress Cataloging-in-Publication Data

McGinn, Peter.
    Leading others, managing yourself / Peter McGinn.
      p. cm.
    Includes bibliographical references.
    ISBN 1-56793-235-5 (alk. paper)
  1. Health services administrators—Psychology. 2. Chief executive officers—Psychology. 3. Executives—Psychology. 4. Health services administration. 5. Executive ability. 6. Leadership. I. Title.

RA971.M4335 2004
362.1'068—dc22

2004059660

The paper used in this publication meets the minimum requirements of American National Standard for Information Sciences—Permanence of Paper for Printed Library Materials, ANSI Z39.48-1984. ∞ ™

Acquisitions editor: Janet Davis; Project manager: Joyce Sherman; Layout editor: Amanda Karvelaitis; Cover design: Trisha Lartz

Health Administration Press
A division of the Foundation of the
   American College of Healthcare Executives
1 North Franklin Street, Suite 1700
Chicago, IL 60606-4425
(312) 424-2800

Introduction

I admit to being a curious professional hybrid. I am a psychologist and the chief executive officer (CEO) of a regional health system. My aim in this book is to share with you some of the lessons I have learned over the past two and a half decades by analyzing the actions of successful leaders and by putting these ideas to the test in my own life.

Over the course of my healthcare and consulting career, I have worked with thousands of managers. I have seen the quest for growth and self-improvement that marks successful executives. Leadership is not just about skills and knowledge; it is also about intuition. Good leaders act, but they also take time for reflection.

This book is for people who seek to build their leadership capabilities and who have the courage to check their assumptions, learn more about themselves, and put their insights into action. The best leaders know themselves, and they know the people with whom they work. Although pressured like everyone else by too many demands and too little time, the most effective leaders know how to manage themselves as well as lead others.

As a healthcare executive, I have faced—and still face every day—the same pressures that confront and challenge you. There are days when, like you, I feel like I am up to my neck in alligators. Over the course of the years, however, I have discovered some basic rules about how things work when people come together to accomplish large tasks and work toward a common mission. These insights have helped me not only to cope with but also to actually enjoy the challenges of leadership. When I keep them in mind, I find I also keep the ups and downs of business in perspective. I am a better leader of others, and I manage my own strengths, skills, and shortcomings better. I hope that will be so for you as well.

In the pages that follow, I have devoted one chapter to each of these basic rules, or "laws." My goal is to give you new ways of looking at some old problems and to help you develop new insights that will make you a better leader. In each chapter, I pose questions to help you reflect a bit more deeply on the key ideas and to promote applications to your own situation.

THE TEN LAWS

- Do the Right Thing: *The First Law of Leadership*
- There Is No *Right* Way: *The First Law of Management*
- Leadership Is an Action, Not a Title: *The Second Law of Leadership*
- Ready...Aim...Fire: *The First Law of Strategy*
- If You Can't Measure It, You Can't Improve It: *The First Law of Measurement*
- If You and I Are Always in Agreement, One of Us Is Not Necessary: *The First Law of Diversity*
- If You Are Coasting, You Are Going Downhill: *The First Law of Competitive Physics*
- One-Dimensional Thinking Is Always Superficial: *The First Law of Analysis*
- If Everyone Is Doing It, Either It Is the Wrong Thing, Or It Is Too Late: *The Second Law of Strategy*
- Stop and Smell the Roses: *The First Law of Executive Stamina*

Figure 1 depicts how these ten laws relate to each other.

The chapters are written from the center moving out toward the rim. Aside from the symbolic importance of having the first law of leadership, "Do the right thing," in the center of the chart, there is no reason other than narrative flow for how close or far from the center each law is placed. There is meaning, however, in the three slices of the chart. The upper right slice focuses primarily on analytical aspects of leadership. The upper left focuses on action and energy. The bottom focuses on lessons that are counterintuitive. Leadership always includes these three factors: analysis, action, and surprises. As you begin each chapter, you may want to refer back to Figure 1 to help reorient yourself to the structure of the whole. The human brain learns best and retains the most information when it is able to put new ideas in context and to relate them to earlier information and experiences.

This is a very short book. You could easily read it all in one evening.

Figure 1. The Ten Laws

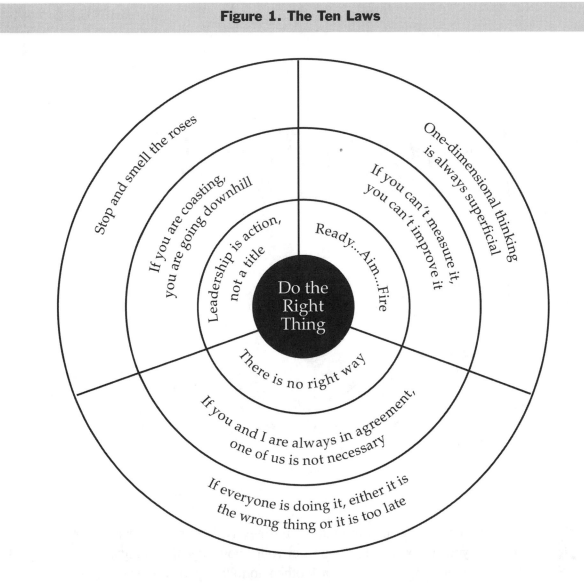

Figure 1. The Ten Laws

- Stop and smell the roses
- One-dimensional thinking is always superficial
- If you are coasting, you are going downhill
- If you can't measure it, you can't improve it
- Leadership is action, not a title
- Ready...Aim...Fire
- Do the Right Thing
- There is no right way
- If you and I are always in agreement, one of us is not necessary
- If everyone is doing it, either it is the wrong thing or it is too late

I suggest, however, that you take your time with it, perhaps reading one chapter per week. People have very limited short-term memories. If you want to get the maximum out of your reading, it is best to work with the material, integrating the content of each chapter into your own thinking before moving on to the next one. After all, this is an investment you are making in yourself. Make it pay off.

CHAPTER 1

Do the Right Thing

The First Law of Leadership

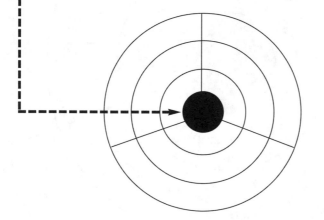

Here it is—first line, no beating around the bush—as a leader, you have a moral obligation to your followers. To the best of your knowledge and ability, you must do the right thing. When you ask others to follow you, you are making an unwritten contract with them. In effect, you are saying, "In return for your loyalty and support, I will work on behalf of our mutual best interests."

Once upon a time, not very long ago, most healthcare managers might dismiss a chapter like this one. "Unnecessary," they would say. "Too obvious." In the last few years, however, too many executives—like those at Enron, Tyco, WorldCom, and Arthur Andersen—have violated this first law of leadership. And they were not alone. ▶

In healthcare, the reckless behavior of the leaders of the Allegheny Health Education and Research Foundation (AHERF), Columbia HCA, Health South, and others created huge problems for their organizations and the communities they serve. For the most part, the CEOs and leading executives of these organizations were admired figures even shortly before their falls from grace. The business and healthcare press touted these leaders' savvy and initiative.

What went wrong? How did people apparently at the top of their game derail so spectacularly? Are there any lessons for the rest of us?

OUR CAPACITY FOR SELF-DECEPTION

Have you ever dieted? Chances are you lied to yourself more than once: "This cake doesn't count because it's Jeff's birthday. I would insult him if I didn't have a piece." "I'm tired, and I deserve a break; eating chocolate doesn't count when I'm tired."

The human capacity for denial and rationalization is both common and extensive. It is not only *possible* to hold two mutually exclusive ideas in our heads at one time and feel no

discomfort but it is also *easy* and natural. The allure of power, public recognition, and financial success can lead managers to make bad choices—when really they know better.

Healthcare leaders, in particular, can suffer from an innocent-looking form of self-deception. Their belief in the purity and goodness of their community-benefit mission may lead them to accept their own behavior uncritically. Few people are so lacking in insight as those who believe in their own inherent moral goodness. Put such self-righteous people together on a hospital management team—or any team— and you have the ingredients for trouble.

So, yes, the first law of leadership may be *obvious*, but it is also *necessary*.

KNOWING RIGHT AND DOING RIGHT ARE NOT THE SAME THING

Sometimes it is easy to *know* what the right thing is, but not always. And sometimes it is easy to *do* the right thing, but again, not always.

A simple 2 × 2 table can help clarify the challenges that the typical healthcare manager faces (Figure 2).

Figure 2. Knowing Versus Doing

		Knowing What Is Right	
		Easy to Know	Hard to Know
Doing What is Right	Easy to Do	Type 1: Easy, obvious action	Type 2: Complex problems with multiple variables
	Hard to Do	Type 3: Hesitation, doubt, or fear	Type 4: Complex dilemmas and conflicts

If it is easy to know what to do and easy to do it, you have a Type 1 situation. For example, a patient brings to your attention an easily fixable problem. It is not a symptom of an underlying system error, just a simple mistake. You correct it. You just do it.

If you face a complex problem with multiple variables, you have a Type 2 situation. You may or may not be able to figure out the solution, if there is one, but your action choices can still be easy to implement. Say your inpatient census has risen, and you are temporarily using overtime and agency personnel to cover the units. Will the current increase in demand continue? Should you add

extra staff? You may not be sure of the right answer, but if you decide to add the staff, the human resources department can do so according to usual procedures.

HESITATION, DOUBT, AND FEAR

But the challenge becomes much tougher in Type 3 situations. You have a Type 3 problem when you find it difficult to act even when you know the right thing to do. Should you enforce a policy that may alienate a big admitter? This is the realm of hesitation, doubt, or fear. You fail to do what you know you should do.

Why? You may face opposing forces or obstacles. You may be pressured by someone else. You may feel tired or afraid. You may lack the will or physical or emotional energy. Perhaps you possess insufficient skill or resources. Possibly, the difficulty comes from competing priorities or conflicts of interest. In any event, when put to the test, you fail to rise to the challenge.

If Type 3 situations can cause hesitation and inaction, Type 4s can create both paralysis and impulsiveness. Complex dilemmas and conflicts can grip you in an emotional vise because no alternative is clear, and the stakes may be high. For example, should you do battle with an important specialty group because it is investing in a competitive venture while still admitting a large minority of its patients to your facility? Paradoxically, Type 4s can also lead to impulsiveness because of the challenge of accurately calculating all of the variables and possibilities.

Good people make mistakes. A short cut here. A compromise there. A wink and a nod. A failure to act. Silence where objections should be made. There are things you can do, however, when faced with Type 3 and 4 problems.

AMBITION, COURAGE, AND SELF-AWARENESS

Ambition is the antidote for hesitation and doubt, and courage is the antidote for fear. Self-awareness is the antidote for ambition and courage run amok.

Ambition has gotten a bad rap. So think of it instead as vision, desire, or purpose. When you are tired or afraid or lack emotional or physical energy, ambition can drive you forward. When Collins (2001) describes "Level 5 leaders" in *Good to Great*, he notes that although personally modest, such leaders were also noteworthy for their great and unwavering ambition on behalf of their organizations and their missions. A sense of purpose and a drive to succeed can help you do the right thing where hesitation and doubt could otherwise lead to failure to act. If you lack sufficient ambition, if you are satisfied with the ordinary, you are likely to withdraw from the fight when the going gets tough. You will fail to obey the first law of leadership, "Do the right thing."

Courage, on the other hand, suffers from a different sort of misunderstanding. We can spot Courage (with a big "C") easily when a firefighter runs into a burning building, but we do not often recognize courage (with a small "c") when managers stand up to pressure, deal with opposition, or make unpopular decisions. But when you do these things, your actions make the statement that you will not be intimidated and that you have the backbone to do the right thing even when it is not convenient.

However, every psychologist knows that all virtues have a "shadow side." The shadows of ambition and courage are narcissism, self-centeredness, and recklessness. *Too much* ambition and courage can lead to just as much violation of the first law of leadership as *too little*. This is why cultivating self-awareness is so critical for every leader. Leaders act, but good leaders also spend time in reflection. If you do not take time for self-reflection and for listening to others, it will be very difficult for you to maintain your balance on the ambition and courage scales.

LEADERSHIP MAKES DEMANDS ON ALL OF WHO YOU ARE

To do the right thing means that you both have to know what the right thing is and commit yourself to it. Leadership is a "full-body exercise." You have to use your head, follow your gut, listen to your heart, and engage your soul. You cannot lead just from the neck up—or just the neck down. Leadership takes thought *and* courage.

Leadership is not just about logic; it is also about intuition. It is about facts, but it is also about feelings. To do the right thing means you have to pay as much attention to "why?" and "why not?" as you do to "what?" and "how?"

ASK YOURSELF

1. Do you know what is important to you? What are the goals or dreams that drive you?
2. How often do you take at least 30 minutes to reflect on your behavior, your tactics, and your decisions? Once a month? Once a week? Less? More?
3. Since the healthcare world is unpredictable, we all make compromises and take risks. Can you identify compromises you have made or risks you are willing to take?
4. When was the last time you discussed ethics with colleagues in the business setting?
5. What are your "hot buttons," the challenges that cause you to react with passion, and possibly with defensiveness?

6. Who do you seek out for feedback? Whose judgment do you trust when it comes to your own behavior?

7. On which kinds of issues do you most trust your logic? On which do you trust your intuition?

LAST WORD

There is a wonderful concept in the law. Lawyers call it a *consideration*. A contract is not valid unless there is some benefit (i.e., a consideration) for each party. If we sign an agreement that calls for you to give me something and I do not give you anything in return, there is no consideration and, therefore, no contract. In terms of leadership, the first, most important, most fundamental consideration you give your followers is to do the right thing to the best of your knowledge and ability.

REFERENCE

Collins, J. 2001. *Good to Great: Why Some Companies Make the Leap...And Others Don't*. New York: HarperCollins.

CHAPTER 2

There Is No *Right* Way

The First Law of Management

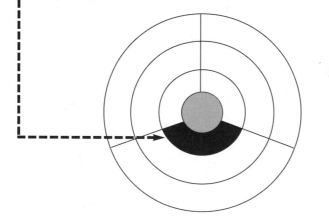

There is no right way. There are only *wrong* ways, and your job as a manager is to choose a path from among all of the wrong ways of doing something. When I initially described this law to my executive MBA students in organizational behavior (OB), they looked at me as if the only thing they had done wrong was to enroll in OB. Perhaps you are experiencing similar feelings right now.

Think of it this way. Just as in physics where every action has an equal and opposite reaction, in management, every action has unintended and/or unanticipated side effects. The first law of management warns you to be alert to side effects. If as a manager you consider only the positive, intended consequences of your actions, you ▶

will experience many unpleasant surprises. That situation is not fun, efficient, or effective.

A LESSON FROM MANAGEMENT CONSULTING

Here is a dirty little secret from the world of management consulting. Often, the easiest way to gain immediate improvements in a decentralized healthcare organization is to recommend centralization, while in a centralized organization, the best advice is to decentralize—exactly the opposite. Why? Because each approach to organization has negative side effects, but the only ones that are obvious are the ones you are living with now. That is why "the grass is always greener on the other side of the fence." I would bet there have been billions of dollars of consultant fees earned this way.

LESSONS FROM ORGANIZATIONAL LIFE CYCLES

I discovered the first law of management when I myself was a management consultant. A colleague of mine, David Merrill, described the life cycle of organizations in a way that allowed me to cut straight to the heart of many of the client problems I encountered (Rohrer, Hibler & Replogle, Inc. 1981).

Merrill showed that every organization goes through predictable stages and that the strengths of each stage are eventually offset by corresponding weaknesses that force organizations to grow or to fail. In other words, each way of organizing contains the seeds of its own crisis. When managers know about these stages, problems, and crises, they can anticipate and react more quickly and intelligently, but they cannot avoid them. What they can do is *choose a path* while understanding that there will be consequences. Under the best of circumstances, they can choose the path whose *consequences they are most willing and able to live with*.

As you read the descriptions that follow, I suspect you will see reflections of your own organization. Within your hospital or health system, you may have business units at different stages of development. You may be experiencing one or another of the crises described. If so, you are likely to be frustrated, impatient, or even angry with the situation and the people you believe to be responsible. Understanding the stages should help you manage the inevitable challenges without attributing them to character flaws or shortcomings within yourself or your colleagues.

The Characteristics and Crises of the Five Stages

THE ENTREPRENEURIAL STAGE The first stage of organizational life begins when entrepreneurs create new products or services with specific competitive advantages. These companies struggle for survival. When they succeed, it is usually through a combination of luck, smarts, and drive—all emanating from the founder. The founder normally keeps his or her hands directly on the reins of the business. The founder is the leader, and everyone else is a follower. Eventually, however, as the company grows, the decisiveness, resourcefulness, and frugality of the entrepreneur cannot overcome the company's lack of planning, systems, capital, and technical depth. This leads to a crisis of leadership.

THE PERSONAL STAGE If the organization can transition power and control from the founder to a top management team, it can maintain the competitive advantage established during the entrepreneurial period. This can be one of the happiest times of an organization's life as it builds strength in its market. The company develops product expertise, team loyalty, and organizational and career stability. Usually, a strong, centralized, top-down management structure is created while traditions are built that reinforce organizational culture and "our way" of doing things. Ultimately, however, innovation slows; traditions become inflexible; inefficiencies abound; and younger, lower-level employees feel ignored and confined. They need opportunities, and the company needs a way to regain its competitive edge. This triggers a crisis of autonomy.

THE PROFESSIONAL STAGE The company's leadership realizes (or is forced to realize) that it needs to become more businesslike and profit oriented and allow decision making closer to the customer. This can be a harsh transition as the "old ways" and "old guard" are forced out. A new performance/reward mentality replaces old concepts of loyalty. Decentralized profit centers replace old functional divisions. Power and responsibility are delegated. There may be competition between business units; indeed, it may even be encouraged. With this comes fractionalization, the loss of synergy, and sometimes shortsightedness. This causes a crisis of control.

THE BUREAUCRATIC STAGE To regain control, the organization develops a centralized staff and systems to ensure that corporate objectives have priority over individual unit goals. Top management pulls resources back to the central organization and implements long-range planning and comprehensive information systems. It monitors performance against clearly stated objectives. Each business unit and subgroup leader is expected to conform to corporate directives. The organization itself becomes rigid and impersonal. Decision making slows down. This stage is characterized by a crisis of red tape.

THE MATRIX STAGE An organization that makes it this far is a large and sophisticated one. It tries to create the best of both worlds by simultaneously centralizing and decentralizing. A centralized functional structure coexists with a decentralized business unit structure. Managers often report to two or more

bosses, for example, their site boss and their functional boss. Decisions are made by those "most qualified" in any given situation. Flexibility, adaptability, and freedom reign. So do complexity, ambiguity, and politics. It becomes very difficult to define and communicate the corporate mission. This precipitates a crisis of purpose.

So what is the *right* way to structure an organization? There is no right way. Each way has negative consequences. As a healthcare leader, you need to understand and anticipate side effects and be prepared to deal with them.

UNINTENDED AND UNANTICIPATED CONSEQUENCES

Lock the following chart in your working memory (Figure 3). It will be your tool for coping with the first law of management.

Every action has unintended and unanticipated consequences. If as a manager you only plan for results in quadrant 1, that is, what you want and what you expect, you will often be frustrated, disappointed, or surprised. Your actions will always lead to unintended consequences in

Figure 3. Table of Consequences

		Anticipated	
		Yes	No
Intended	Yes	1 Intended and anticipated	2 Hoped for but not assured
	No	3 Unwanted but expected	4 Neither wanted nor expected

addition to those outcomes you desire. If you allow the possibility of such consequences into your thinking, you can make better choices—often more creative and insightful ones. You will be prepared for the inevitable variances from plan.

ASK YOURSELF

1. What mechanisms do you have set up to ensure that you consider side effects of planned actions?
2. Do you encourage or discourage those who play the devil's advocate role in your organization?
3. Do you play that role also? When?

4. When was the last time you got caught by a mistaken impression that the "grass is greener on the other side"?
5. In what stage of the organizational life cycle is your department, division, or healthcare organization now? How are you managing the inevitable problems?
6. How do you balance autonomy for your direct reports with the need to exercise control and gain efficiencies?
7. Do you ever use formal decision-making tools like performance improvement or continuous quality improvement to help improve your consideration of alternatives?

LAST WORD

In complex decision making, groups usually perform better than individuals because of the range of skills and breadth of perspectives represented within the group. There is a major exception, however, when group members prematurely settle on a single course of action. They achieve a state of *groupthink* and become remarkably resistant to the consideration of any alternatives (Janis 1982). Groupthink can help hospital senior management teams or medical staff organizations achieve failures as notorious in their own world as the Bay of Pigs invasion debacle in American foreign policy. Remember the first law of management: there is no right way. By considering the possible consequences of your decisions, you can short-circuit groupthink in your organization.

REFERENCES

Janis, I. 1982. *Groupthink: Psychological Studies of Policy Decisions and Fiascos*, 2nd ed. Boston: Houghton Mifflin.

Rohrer, Hibler & Replogle, Inc. 1981. *The Managerial Challenge: A Psychological Approach to the Changing World of Management*. New York: The New American Library.

CHAPTER 3

Leadership Is an Action, Not a Title

The Second Law of Leadership

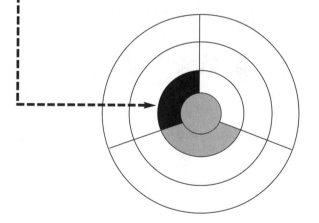

Whether you are a first-line supervisor or a CEO, your title carries weight with others. Both inside and outside the organization, the people you meet assume that you have earned your position. They credit you with a certain level of skill and drive before knowing much else about you. It is almost like a *free pass*, but not quite. You must live up to their expectations or lose credibility quickly. The ceremonial and symbolic roles of leaders are important, but ▶

they do not replace action. You gain influence and legitimacy by what you do, not by the title on your name badge.

ACTIONS SPEAK

Dr. Robert Heyssel piloted the Johns Hopkins Health System through the 1980s and into the 1990s. Bob had a reputation for foresight and decisiveness. He was a giant among healthcare leaders, and I was fortunate to serve as Hopkins' vice president for human resources during the last two years before his retirement. One day I complained to him that our employee benefits programs were based on a faulty economic and healthcare model. He asked a few questions to understand my thinking and then said, "Well then, why don't you change the benefits structure to make it right?" To him, it was the most natural approach. If something needs fixing, fix it. If it can be done better, do it. His bias for action propelled Hopkins forward during his tenure.

Another person in a similar situation, leading a high-profile institution like Hopkins, might be more interested in the public status that the position offers. As I discovered when I was a vice president at Hopkins, the association of Hopkins' name with mine gave me immediate credibility when discussing issues with colleagues from other hospitals. That type of recognition provides a great platform for action, but it can easily be wasted. If you want your department, division, or organization to continue to move forward, you must be ready and willing to do the hard work of management. If you want to make an impact, your actions must speak as loudly as your words. Leadership is an action, not a title.

DRIVING FROM THE BACK OF THE BUS

Leadership does not just apply to CEOs, however. Try this: picture the inside of a moving bus. You see a driver with a handful of passengers. The driver is working, and everyone else is along for the ride—talking, reading, sleeping, or looking out the windows. That model works fine for mass transit, but it does not work in healthcare. Any organization where the only leadership comes from the top and everyone else is along for the ride is an organization headed for trouble. Although a CEO has a lot of organizational power, he or she is not the only one with motivation, skills, relationships, intelligence, and ideas. The CEO is not the only driver.

In your organization, you can help drive the bus regardless of where you sit, if you think and act like a leader. If you want to implement an idea for change, you must take responsibility for building it into a real action opportunity. If you are going to drive, not just be a passenger, you cannot pass along a half-baked idea. You need to develop it and identify potential costs and impacts. You must align it with corporate strategy and build support for it. Busses do not drive themselves, and ideas do not implement themselves. An impressive title does not ensure that you will help your organization progress, but right action does.

THINKING ONE LEVEL UP

To further magnify your impact and your ability to influence the direction of your organization, follow this advice: *Make it a point to think about the problems and opportunities of the organization from the perspective of those at the next higher level of management or supervision.* If you

are a staff member, how do weekend scheduling problems look to your supervisor? If you are a nurse manager, how do overtime issues look to the chief nursing officer? If you are a CEO, how do hospital billing practices look to a board member, a legislator, or the public?

Thinking one level up will put you in a frame of mind to determine what action to take to seize an opportunity or resolve a problem. It will move you from being a passive observer or victim to becoming a doer. It will aid your understanding of the situation as you work with your peers and your supervisor. Your actions are more likely to contribute to overall progress and fit better with the efforts of others when you take this broader perspective. You are less likely to misread others' intentions. Your authority may be limited by your designated title, but you need not similarly limit your thinking or your ability to contribute because of it.

"LEADING UP"

Michael Useem, director of the Center for Leadership and Change Management at the Wharton School of the University of Pennsylvania, has taken this same concept and described its application in real-life examples (Useem 2001). His stories range from commanding Civil War armies to climbing Mount Everest. *Upward leaders*, as Useem calls them, help their organizations and bosses perform better. In some cases, they achieve things the bosses could not imagine. In other cases, they help avert disaster. As Useem says, you do not have to be in charge to take charge. Or, as the second law of leadership implies, your actions—not your title—are the mark of your leadership.

To lead upward, you need to motivate and encourage those above you, not just those who report to you. In addition, you must establish credibility with your superiors, so that they will listen when you talk. You do this by showing initiative, sharing vital information, and helping them succeed. And as Chapter 1 urges, you exercise courage and honesty to do the right thing. Useem points out that "getting an unwanted message up to the top can be one of the most challenging but also one of the most important actions for an upward leader" (Useem 2001, 102–103).

Leading upward is most effective when you understand the organization's overall mission and your boss's immediate intentions. If you do detailed work and build a factual foundation that enables your boss to make good decisions in difficult situations, you are helping steer the organization. You are leading up, driving from the back of the bus, taking action, and making an impact.

ASK YOURSELF

1. Who are your leadership role models who display a bias for action? How can you emulate them better?

2. Who are some people in your organization who have an impact greater than their title would suggest? How do they do it?

3. What organizational problems, issues, or opportunities are most important to your boss? How can you help?

4. What do you know that your boss needs to know but does not? How can you improve your boss's ability to make good decisions?

5. When have you been most successful in influencing the direction of your department, division, or organization? How did you do it?

6. Are there problems or "unwanted messages" in your organization

that are being covered over because no one has the courage to bring them to light? What can you do about that?

7. How can you create a better environment for the people who report to you so that they can help you with *your* organizational problems, issues, and opportunities and so that they can help you make better decisions?

LAST WORD

Bill George, former CEO of Medtronic, proposes that "leadership begins and ends with *authenticity*" (George 2003, 11). To become an authentic leader,

> it is essential that you first answer the question, 'Leadership for what purpose?' If you lack purpose and direction in leading, why would anyone want to follow you? Many people want to become leaders without giving much thought to their purpose. They are attracted to the power and prestige of leading an organization and the financial rewards that go with it. But without a real sense of purpose, leaders are at the mercy of their egos.... (George 2003, 19)

Leaders in healthcare have an advantage because the nature of the work naturally aligns itself with core human values, but even so, an authentic leader needs to reaffirm purpose through words and actions.

To create a lasting impact on your organization, you want to become a leader in fact, not a leader just in title. Ceremonies and symbolism have a legitimate and valuable role in encouraging staff and confirming organizational priorities. But your authenticity and accomplishments give you legitimacy and credibility as a leader of others.

REFERENCES

George, B. 2003. *Authentic Leadership: Rediscovering the Secrets to Creating Lasting Value*. San Francisco: Jossey-Bass.

Useem, M. 2001. *Leading Up: How to Lead Your Boss So You Both Win*. New York: Crown Business.

CHAPTER 4

Ready…Aim…Fire

The First Law of Strategy

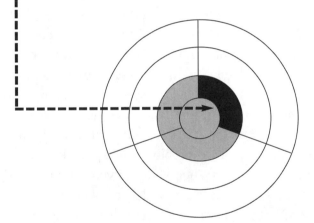

When you are up to your neck in alligators, it is hard to remember that your original intention was to drain the swamp. You hurtle from one crisis to another. When you stop to catch your breath, you find another few months have passed. Your to-do list is no shorter, and strategic priorities still await your focused attention and action. Instead of "ready…aim…fire," your approach is "fire…fire…fire…."

You are in a spin cycle. To get out of it, you need some tools. ▶

THE S-T-P MODEL

When I was young, an octane enhancer called STP promoted itself as "the racer's edge." Years later, a consulting colleague, Joe McGill, taught me about another STP that was even more powerful. McGill's S-T-P model is a great tool for effective problem solving. In this model, *S = Situation*, *T = Target*, and *P = Proposal*. S-T-P reminds you to clarify where you are and where you intend to go before you decide how to get there. It seems so simple, but many smart people behave otherwise.

Not long ago, I was in a large roundtable discussion with healthcare leaders that reminded me of the power of S-T-P. The question concerned the vacuum in community health planning that has been created by the demise of the health systems agencies around the country. Various interest groups are competing to fill that planning role, including insurers, business coalitions, government agencies, and politicians. The discussion identified potential problems that could be created by any of these groups exerting inappropriate or harmful controls. Members offered multiple suggestions of ways to prevent that

from happening. We were dealing with our situation and proposals for action, and we were going nowhere fast.

Finally, after prolonged debate, one of our members suggested that we first identify the core principals that we sought to achieve relative to community health planning. Then we could identify alternatives and evaluate them in light of these core principals. In other words, we had agreement on the situation (S), but *before* we could logically discuss proposals for action (P), we needed clarity on just what we wanted to achieve (T). By helping us apply S-T-P in the right order, he got us out of the spin cycle and put us back on a good problem-solving track.

When you find yourself in one of those group debates where the discussion seems to be going in circles, check to see if S-T-P can help. If your organization or department seems to have lost its way or if actions are poorly coordinated or contradictory, you need S-T-P.

First, clarify whether you have agreement on what the problem or situation is. Can you describe it in a couple of sentences that everyone can endorse? That is "S."

Next, do the same for your goal. Describe your intended outcome or

Figure 4. Vision and Action

		Vision	
		No	*Yes*
Action	*High*	1 Going nowhere fast	2 Full speed ahead
	Low	3 Adrift	4 "The vision thing": No action/ talk only

target in a few sentences and test for agreement. That is "T," your desired endpoint.

Only then can you begin to identify ways of getting from where you are now (situation) to where you want to be (target). Those are your proposals. From among these alternatives, choose the one that becomes your "P."

If you can make S-T-P a habit or preferred problem-solving tool in your group, you are likely to experience a greatly enhanced sense of progress and efficiency. S-T-P is another way of saying, "ready...aim...fire." Try it.

VISION

When George Bush (the elder) was campaigning for president, he criticized what he called "the vision thing." He wanted to contrast action and words, the difference between doing things and just talking about them. That is an important distinction, but it is also true that a vision can help direct and propel action.

A 2 × 2 chart can help you sort out the interaction of vision and action (Figure 4).

When vision and action work together, they are a powerful combination, allowing "full speed ahead." When either is missing, the results suffer greatly. Vision without action is ineffectual talking ("the vision thing"). Action without vision is meaningless or misdirected activity. When both are missing, you are quite literally adrift. Progress results from a combination of vision and action—when, in Covey's words, you "begin with the end in mind" (Covey 1990).

PERSONAL AND ORGANIZATIONAL MISSION STATEMENTS

Covey advocates that each organization, each group, each family, and each individual create a mission statement. From many years in healthcare management, I knew about the value of organizational mission statements. When I first read Covey's book *The Seven Habits of Highly Effective People* (1990), however, I was a skeptic about personal mission statements. Since then, experience has made me a believer.

As a convert to the concept of personal mission statements, I now preach to others about their value. Too many healthcare leaders assume that the intrinsic worth of their chosen vocation makes that type of self-reflection unnecessary. They believe that good intentions are good enough. Just as in organizational life, however, personal mission statements combined with action increase both effectiveness and satisfaction. If you want to produce a personal mission statement, there are seven steps to take.

1. Identify the things that you enjoy most and are best at doing.
2. Write down the values that are most important to you.
3. Edit those two lists, removing the items that are there to impress others.
4. Test each of the remaining items by asking yourself "why?" for each one, so that you can get to the most fundamental goals or core values that drive you.
5. Write and rewrite a mission statement based on those ideas until you can get a draft that is compelling and motivating for you—and that is no longer than 25 words.
6. Share this statement with people close to you and consider their feedback carefully.
7. Repeat steps 1 through 6 as necessary.

When you follow this process, you are applying the first law of strategy "ready...aim...fire" to your most important project: your own life.

ASK YOURSELF

1. When you are up to your neck in alligators, what techniques have you found that help *you* regain focus and control?
2. Does your work group ever feel like it is either drifting or going nowhere fast? Does it have a clearly stated and accepted target?
3. Would a vision or mission statement help your work group make better choices or work together more effectively?

THE FINE PRINT

WARNING: The Surgeon General has determined that life does not always work out as expected. Addiction to plans may cause inflexibility and missed opportunities. Plans may have undesired side effects. In rapidly changing or competitive environments, frequent adjustments may be required. In addition, the goals and plans of other people and organizations may interact with your own. Plans cannot fully account for the operation of luck, coincidence, acts of nature, or the hand of God. Be prepared to discontinue or alter plans as appropriate for your circumstances.

4. Do you have a personal mission? Is it written? Could you say it or write it in 25 words or less?

5. What specific things do you plan to accomplish this week? What are your most important objectives for the next 90 days? Do they fit with your personal mission?

6. Has your personal or organizational mission changed? How did you know?

7. What are some circumstances in which flexibility or adaptability served you better than did a plan?

THE LAST WORD

When you think of the first law of strategy, you should also consider it the first law of *time management*. Figure 4 is also a time management chart. All of the time management tools that help you avoid interruptions, organize work, and become more efficient are just so much wasted effort if you are heading in the wrong direction. You simply get nowhere faster. The best time management tools begin with the end in mind. See, for example, the classics: *How to Get Control of Your Time and Your Life* (Lakein 1974) and *First Things First* (Covey, Merrill, and Merrill 1995). When you combine vision and action—while remaining open to change—you can achieve the greatest results and derive the most satisfaction in the limited amount of time that you can call your own.

REFERENCES

Covey, S. R. 1990. *The Seven Habits of Highly Effective People: Restoring the Character Ethic*. New York: Simon & Schuster.

Covey, S. R., A. R. Merrill, and R. R. Merrill. 1995. *First Things First: To Live, to Love, to Learn, to Leave a Legacy*. New York: Simon & Schuster.

Lakein, A. 1974. *How to Get Control of Your Time and Your Life*. New York: Penguin.

CHAPTER 5

If You Can't Measure It, You Can't Improve It

The First Law of Measurement

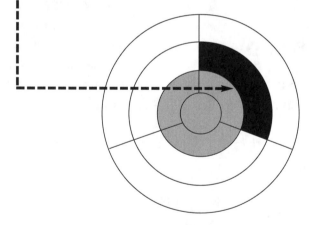

Former U.S. Senator Bill Bradley (D-New Jersey) was an unusually gifted basketball player, but how he worked his game provides lessons for all of us—and not just in sports. From his high school years right through his professional career with the New York Knicks, he practiced relentlessly. He spent hours each day and took hundreds of shots to improve his skill and control. But just imagine for a moment how utterly useless all of his practice would have been if he could not see the basket after he released the ball. ▶

What if a screen hid the basket from his eyes so he could not see when he hit and when he missed? What if he received no visual feedback to help make adjustments higher or lower, left or right? What if he could not even count how many baskets and how many misses he had overall? He would not have gotten better. He would not have had fun. And there would have been no point to his practice.

Why should you think that healthcare management is any different? How can you get better if you cannot measure progress, identify your mistakes, make adjustments, and measure again? Beethoven could write a symphony when he was deaf, but that was after a lifetime of immersion in music—and he was a genius. Perhaps you and I, too, can manage without measurements, *after* a lifetime of outstanding accomplishments and *if* we are geniuses.

When I see healthcare leaders and organizations struggling, it is often because they have neglected the proper role of measurement. They are literally out of control because they have no objective data to assess their progress. Without the feedback that measurement provides, you have no basis for making adjustments or fine-tuning your actions. Just as you cannot play a sport if the goal is hidden from you, or improve your musical skill without auditory feedback, you cannot manage without tools for evaluating progress. You can only make the grossest of judgments in the most obvious of situations. That is the plight of managers in organizations where measures are too few, too imprecise, or undervalued.

LESSONS FROM REENGINEERING

Back in the "old days"—in the last decade of the previous century—the reengineering craze swept through management circles in healthcare and general business. At that time, managers were struggling to regain a sense of progress and productivity. Reengineering tapped into widespread concern about lagging performance in the competitive marketplace. It promised a radical way to restructure the way business was done in this country.

The leading guru of reengineering was Michael Hammer, who preached process simplification and measurement (Hammer and Champy 1993). He argued that business processes need to be torn apart and redesigned from scratch with measurements of key objectives guiding the process. Hammer drove home his message with a mantra consisting of three verses: If you can't define it, you can't measure it. If you can't measure it, you can't manage it. And if you can't manage it, you can't improve it. Hammer's three-part formula can help you assess opportunities for improvements in your own organization.

In healthcare, as in business generally, fuzzy objectives lead to absent, imprecise, or invalid measurements. How many hospital mission statements have you read that proclaim their intention to improve *the health of the community*? How many vision statements declare an aspiration to be *the best*? How many of those organizations have defined what they mean by "the health of the community" or "the best"? Not defining or being able to define your goals is like playing a game without knowing how score is kept.

Kaplan and Norton (1996) have taken these reengineering concepts and applied them to strategy. According to Kaplan and Norton, you need to define your key objectives in measurable terms and link them in a cause and effect chain. What you measure should reflect your theory of what makes your organization or

your department effective. Then you can focus your efforts in those critical few areas that make the most difference. Measurement becomes one of your chief management tools. You define your goals in measurable terms, you track them, and you make adjustments based on the results. Measurement is not an add-on, but rather is at the core of your management actions. Remember, if you can't measure it, you can't improve it.

"MONEYBALL"

First, however, you must determine the *right* things to measure. Here, a story from the world of major league baseball is instructive. In an era of free agency and high salaries, how can teams from smaller metropolitan areas compete with the big-budget teams from New York and Los Angeles? That is the question of *Moneyball: The Art of Winning an Unfair Game*, by Michael Lewis (2003). It is the story of the 2002 Oakland A's, who had both the lowest payroll in major league baseball and one of the highest winning percentages.

How did they do it? Billy Beane, the general manager of the A's, had a theory of baseball that differed from most of his peers, and he measured different things: percentage on base rather than batting average, for example. Beane rated walks higher than sacrifice flies. Neither counts in a player's official average, but one gets a player on base without an out, and the other advances a runner but at the cost of an out. Beane defined what was important. He created measurement systems to track those statistics. Then he enforced a discipline to those measures with his scouts, his manager and coaches, and his players. As a result, his team of Davids was competitive with any team of Goliaths that major league baseball could field.

Again, how did they do it? They studied the core measurements in their business until they understood what makes a difference and what does not, and they acted on what they learned. You should, too.

BREAKTHROUGH MEASURES

There is one more lesson on measurement that can help you, if you are ready to challenge yourself and your organization to go beyond the ordinary: *breakthrough measures*.

I learned about breakthrough measures from Universal Instruments, a company in the highly competitive marketplace of chip manufacturing. To succeed in that environment, they had used breakthrough measures to turbocharge the rule of measure, manage, and improve. Breakthrough measures are those targets that take you to a dramatically new level of performance. If you currently earn a 5 percent margin on a particular service line and improve that to 7 percent, that is incremental improvement. If you double your margin to 10 percent, that is a stretch. If you improve it to 40 percent, or 70 percent, or 100 percent, *that* is a breakthrough.

Breakthrough measures work because they undermine status quo thinking. You deliberately set measures that cannot be achieved by conventional means. You dare yourself and your team to let go of your traditional approaches and create totally new ways of reaching your goal. You use breakthrough measurements as the tool to frame the challenge.

Universal Instruments used breakthrough measures to unfreeze their thinking and unleash their creativity. They identified barriers that would prevent accomplishment of their objectives and brainstormed ways to overcome each one. They used their breakthrough measures to track their progress and achieved operational and bottom-line performance far above previous results.

When you apply the first law of management in your organization, remember the lesson of Universal Instruments: Think bold; think *breakthrough*.

ASK YOURSELF

1. Which measures do you track most closely in your work to monitor your overall progress?
2. Which measures serve as your early warning indicators to signal that trouble may be developing?
3. Do you use a balanced scorecard? Are the measures independent or linked in a cause and effect chain?
4. In your organization, is measurement a core management tool or a burdensome paperwork exercise?
5. As general manager of the Oakland A's, Billy Beane employed measures that reflected fresh insights into the dynamics of baseball. Do any of your measures reflect fresh insights into the dynamics of healthcare?
6. Do you have opportunities for achieving significant forward progress by challenging yourself and your team with breakthrough objectives instead of incremental improvements?
7. Have you made mistakes with measurement? Used the wrong measures? Used too many or too few? Collected data but did not use it?

LAST WORD

I believe in the power of measurement. Not only do I believe but I also preach it to others. In my organization, I can often hear a manager quoting me to others: "If you can't measure it, you can't manage it." But when I hear that, I sometimes cringe. Why? Because I also believe what Einstein said: "Not everything that *counts* can be counted." As much as I believe in measurement, I also know that measurement is only a tool and not an end in itself.

Do not make the mistake of confusing your measures with your ultimate mission itself. Step back from your measures every now and again and ask how your measures are helping you improve performance. Einstein also said, "Not everything that can be counted counts."

REFERENCES

Hammer, M., and J. Champy. 1993. *Reengineering the Corporation: A Manifesto for Business Revolution*. New York: Harper Business.

Kaplan, R., and D. Norton. 1996. *The Balanced Scorecard: Translating Strategy into Action*. Boston: Harvard Business School Publishing.

Lewis, M. 2003. *Moneyball: The Art of Winning an Unfair Game*. New York: W.W. Norton.

CHAPTER 6

If You and I Are Always in Agreement, One of Us Is Not Necessary

The First Law of Diversity

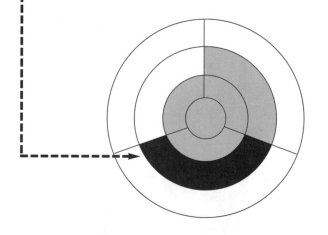

U nited Health Services, the organization I currently head, was formed through the merger of three independent hospitals in 1981 and went through a turbulent adjustment for at least the next five years. The founding CEO brought together three disparate cultures, hired new senior management, and ▶

left two years later. A new CEO was hired in 1984. He began to bring in his own team and hired me as a consultant to help deal with the clash of skills, styles, and culture among senior management.

I facilitated an off-site retreat that first year and witnessed the corrosive effect of lack of trust and competing agendas. The group even had trouble working together on simple team simulation exercises. Not only was there overt conflict but also their problem-solving scores were quite low. Over the course of the following year, the CEO added several new members to senior management and worked hard to create a high-performance team. I again facilitated the annual off-site retreat and once more included team simulation exercises. The overt conflict was gone. Participants deferred to one another. They consistently chose agreement over conflict. However, I was in for a surprise. On the problem-solving tests, their scores were even worse than the poor scores senior management had achieved the previous year.

We all learned an important lesson: too much agreement can be as harmful to good teamwork as too little. That insight helped the members adjust their behavior and become an energized, productive, and creative team that balanced agreement and disagreement. *If you and I are always in agreement, one of us is not necessary.*

LESSONS FROM SPORTS

It is even easier to see this phenomenon operating in team sports. Visualize the players on a typical team. You will see significant physical differences corresponding to the roles each plays. On a basketball team, for example, the center will typically use height as an advantage both to score on offense and to intimidate the opposition on defense. The power forward will use size and strength to establish and hold position for inside shooting and rebounding. The point guard will rely on speed, agility, and stamina to direct the offense and to disrupt the play of the other team when on defense. Except under the most unusual circumstances, you will not see a basketball team place all of its tallest players on the court simultaneously, or all of its fastest, or its strongest, etc.

A good coach may employ unusual combinations to confuse and defeat the opposition, but it will always be a blend of talents. The team gets its competitive advantage from the diverse skills of its members and the ways that it deploys them. When you watch a good coach in action, you see a person who capitalizes on and manages to the strengths of each team member. The coach treats the players not as interchangeable parts but as unique individuals. In the ebb and flow of the game, the coach makes substitutions to create the team best suited to the challenges of the moment.

DIVERSITY AND PROBLEM SOLVING

You can see the same phenomenon I observed in the early years of United Health Services if you watch problem-solving teams at work in your healthcare organization. For example, if there is low trust, competing agendas, or interpersonal conflict between departments or among senior management, it is hard to get sufficient cooperation for work that requires give and take. If there is premature agreement based on a desire to avoid conflict, it is hard to get a sufficient dialog and range of ideas.

Using the Myers-Briggs Type Indicator or one of the comparable workplace psychological inventories,

you can see this even more clearly. The Myers-Briggs measures for two perceptual preferences (sensing and intuition) and two judging preferences (thinking and feeling). Each person will have a blend of preferences (e.g., sensing and thinking, intuition and feeling, etc.), but one of these four will be dominant. In Myers-Briggs terms, a senser has greater recognition of facts, and an intuitive has more appreciation of possibilities. Similarly, a thinker evaluates things logically, and a feeler makes choices from a values orientation. Put similar Myers-Briggs types together in a problem-solving scenario and you are likely to have much less success than if you create a team with a blend of preferences.

Here is how it might look in action. Recall the S-T-P model from Chapter 4. Good problem solving begins with a description of the current situation, a task that requires the strength of the senser, who can dig in and identify facts. For example, what is happening with market share in specific service lines? Which physicians are shifting volume? An intuitive, however, can do a better job on the next two steps: identifying possible targets and suggesting potential alternative proposals, such as increasing marketing, improving workflow, investing in facilities, or cutting

Figure 5. The STARS Model of Teamwork

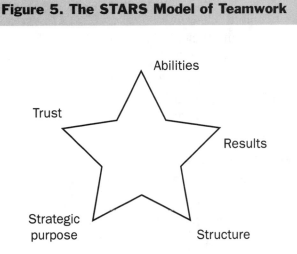

capacity. A thinker would evaluate the strengths and weaknesses of the options under consideration and be able to summarize the advantages and disadvantages of each. Which alternatives have the highest risk, the fastest payback, the most upfront investment? A feeler would ask how these options fit with the mission of the group and help make a selection most in tune with the group's values. For example, does an aggressive, competitive approach fit the role of your hospital in your community?

This is an oversimplified picture, since the individual members are not each pure types, of course. However, if you watch the work of a good team, you will see different members call on their strengths to contribute to team process just as the different members of a sports team do. Like a good coach, a good healthcare leader assembles a team with diverse talents to call on as needed.

DIVERSITY AND TEAMWORK

Diversity on a team provides a greater breadth of talents and perspectives than would be true with a homogeneous group of people. It offers the potential for greater creativity and adaptability. However, if people with different skills, interests, preferences, and backgrounds are just thrown together, inertia or conflict are more likely than progress. Diversity does not convey an automatic advantage for teams; it is something that needs to be managed. An old *Far Side* cartoon shows a jumble of men and horses on the ground with an Old West saloon behind them. Looking over the pile, a sheriff comments to his deputy, "Johnson, you can't just throw it together; a posse is something you have to organize."

I use a STARS model to describe the key attributes of an effective team (Figure 5).

If you read the figure in a clockwise circle starting from the lower left, the initial letters spell out the acronym STARS. These words identify the key aspects for creating effective teams. You start with the left leg, *strategic purpose*, and clarify why the team exists. Then you go to the top of the diagram and select people with the range of *abilities* to accomplish the task. Next, you attend to the other leg of the star by creating a *structure* to organize these diverse talents (a posse is not something you can just throw together…). That leaves the two arms of the star: results and trustworthiness. *Results* are the short-term targets you set that help you and each team member measure your progress toward your strategic purpose. *Trustworthiness* is the way you and other team members behave that demonstrates that you each take responsibility to work toward your common goals. The head of the star highlights the need for diversity. The arms and legs show you how to manage it effectively.

DIVERSITY AND ADAPTABILITY

With all of these benefits of diversity, there is also a drawback. It may be more difficult for you to establish a sense of partnership and a common vision with people who vary too

greatly from one another. It takes longer to pull diverse individuals together into an efficient, smoothly running team. You will find more opinions at odds with one another. You will have unexpected clashes of style and perspective. Team members will take too much for granted with respect to the universality of their own values while at the same time misreading each other's words, actions, and intentions. Think of how hard it is to get surgeons and family practitioners to set common priorities for funding. That is the challenge of diversity.

However, there is another benefit, as yet unmentioned, that outweighs any disadvantages when you are in an environment of great change. Naturalists, who study the adaptation of species, will tell you that the species that are most perfectly adapted to their current environment are the ones least likely to survive when the environment changes. Diversity within a species confers a greater ability to adjust to new circumstances.

In healthcare, as in the natural world, diversity equates to adaptability. In an unstable environment, flexibility serves an organization much better than rigidity. In the political and economic environment of healthcare, you will want to capitalize on the advantages of diversity. By assembling a team with a range of experiences, skills, styles, and viewpoints, you will be able to adjust better and more quickly than your competitors to changing demands, resources, or rewards. If, however, you build an organization of immediately compatible, like-minded people, you will be slow to recognize trends, identify alternatives, and make changes. In healthcare, where change is a constant, diversity should be one of your strategies for success. As the law of diversity warns, too much agreement is not a good thing.

ASK YOURSELF

1. Have you been in situations where mistrust and hidden agendas generated conflict that sapped the energy from a team and hindered effective problem solving and group effort?

2. Have you been in situations where homogeneity or conflict avoidance generated pressure for premature agreement that sapped the flexibility and creativity from a team and hindered effective problem solving and innovation?

3. On your team, whom do you rely on for practicality? For innovation? For logical analysis? For good judgment?

4. In what ways are differences among your team obstacles to progress? What can you do to manage the team more effectively to capitalize on rather than suffer from those differences?

5. With whom do you have a relationship that thrives based on differences of personality, skills, and background? What else sustains the relationship?

6. Can you identify some business successes that were enabled by insights or assessments far different from your own?

7. In what ways are you different from your boss, colleagues, or direct reports? How do your unique talents contribute to team effectiveness?

LAST WORD

One day I joined three staff members for lunch in the hospital cafeteria. When I arrived, they were discussing the new boyfriend of a fourth coworker who was not present. "They are so different. I can't imagine them together. I wonder what they have in common." It happened that I knew that each of my lunch colleagues had been married for more than 20 years, so I asked them how similar each one was to his or her spouse. "Oh, not at all!" they all laughed.

I had anticipated that would be the answer. *Complementarity* is the secret behind many successful relationships. The deepest relationships and the most effective partnerships often involve pairs of opposites, where complementarity is a key virtue.

When you develop a serious partnership in a business or a personal setting, you resonate best with those whose personality attributes fill in gaps in your own spectrum. Complementarity with a partner ensures that the two of you are more than twice as effective as either of you alone. Look at the enduring and effective business or personal partnerships around you. I bet you will find complementarity is a common but unanticipated component of their success.

CHAPTER 7

If You Are Coasting, You Are Going Downhill

The First Law of Competitive Physics

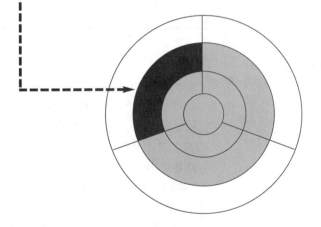

Not long ago, a friend invited me to join him on a long bike ride in the Endless Mountains region of northeast Pennsylvania. "Endless Mountains"—talk about two words designed not to inspire confidence in a cyclist. However, the ride was fabulous: backcountry roads, few cars, rolling hills, and terrific views. The only price to be paid was to follow each exhilarating descent with a long climb up the next hill. As we crested each one, we relaxed for a moment on the downhill side and allowed gravity to do some of the work. We would pick up speed, ▶

our tires would barely hold contact with the ground, and the combination of momentum and furious pedaling would carry us halfway up the next hill before we needed to shift gears for the remainder of the climb.

If healthcare was like biking, downhills would be exciting; declines would always be followed by upturns; and the more downward momentum, the better. You could work hard when you wished, and you could coast when you were tired. Coasting would be an ideal way for you to conserve energy while still making forward progress.

The comparison does not work very well. Although healthcare management can be fun and stimulating, like biking, it is hard to imagine when coasting downhill could correctly be considered progress. Complacency would be a more accurate term.

COMPLACENCY

Two kinds of hospitals and executives become complacent: those who are overconfident and those who do not have a clue (Figure 6).

Zone 3: Overconfidence
The administrators of successful hospitals sometimes begin to lose

Figure 6. Complacency

		Current Success	
		Yes	No
Effort	Energized	1 Success breeds success	2 Revitalization and turnaround
	Coasting	3 The complacency of overconfidence	4 The complacency of cluelessness

their edge. You can see it first appear as a sense that their success is the well-deserved payoff for good work *completed*. They seem to have forgotten the original effort that brought them to the top of the hill.

However, the momentum of success can carry you forward just so long. When you believe that the future will be just like the present, you are like the biker on a long downhill slope who does not understand that there will be more climbs ahead. You do not anticipate the level of exertion required once your forward momentum dissipates. It is as if you have been taken in by your own press clippings. You forget that in addition to your brilliance, your impeccable judgment, your management finesse, and your charisma, continued success also requires sustained effort, focus, and good fortune.

Tom Royer, M.D., CEO of Christus Health in Irving, Texas, provides an instructive contrast to overconfidence. When Tom was CEO of the Henry Ford Medical Group in Detroit, Michigan, he showed how an effective leader could build on success and avoid complacency. In the mid-1990s, the Henry Ford Health System had put together the pieces of an integrated system as well as anyone in the country. Nevertheless, Tom remained highly energized. He continued to seek out ways that service could be improved. He listened carefully to the concerns of individual patients even while collecting national awards and receiving praise from colleagues. Tom graciously hosted me when I visited Henry Ford to learn how it had progressed so quickly and had engaged medical staff as partners. I learned that, like one of the Level 5 leaders described in *Good to Great* (Collins 2001), Tom combined passionate drive with personal modesty. I still recall him commenting near the end of my visit,

"If we continue to work very, very hard, and if we are very, very lucky, someday we will deserve all of the awards we have already won." He never fell victim to overconfidence and a false sense of security but stayed focused on mission and purpose. The work yet to be accomplished continued to motivate him.

Zone 4: Cluelessness

When you observe healthcare organizations slipping into a spiral of decline, you expect top management to ratchet up their energy level, rally the troops, and seek to reverse direction. Unfortunately, many leaders and organizations do not recognize that they have been going downhill until very late in the game.

The Lehigh Gorge Rail Trail is a perfect metaphor for this situation. It runs 25 miles from White Haven, Pennsylvania, to the small town of Jim Thorpe, Pennsylvania. Traveling from north to south, you get the benefit of an almost imperceptible 3 percent downhill gradient. When you bike in that direction, you feel strong and fit. When I take friends on that trail, I have to warn them to turn around for the return trip long before they begin to feel tired. As compared to a 3 percent downhill gradient, a 3 percent *uphill* gradient is immediately noticeable. The contrast is much greater than you would expect. When you are going downhill in the Lehigh Gorge, you do not see the slope at all. You are coasting without realizing it. You take credit for the work that gravity is doing. In effect, you are *clueless* as to the real dynamics at play in your ride.

You can see this at work when hospitals begin to lose market share or financial strength. Managers who are not tracking results carefully seem not to recognize the warning signs of decline. You hear them make statements like, "We've been through worse than this before. This is nothing to get concerned about." They talk more about grand concepts and less about the fundamental blocking and tackling needed to get them back into the game. They are coasting down the equivalent of the Lehigh Gorge Rail Trail when they should be turning around and recognizing that every mile will come at the cost of extra effort. In a sense, they do not recognize the gravity of their situation. They do not understand that "If you are coasting, you are going downhill." In healthcare, you need to stay on top of your game or you will lose ground quickly even if it is not obvious at first. You need ways to keep your organization and your management staff sharp.

PURPOSE AND PASSION

How can you create a culture of performance? The best leaders, the ones who make a difference, always use impact as their measure of success. They create a compelling vision for themselves and their followers and push themselves to overcome all obstacles to reach their goals.

Purpose provides direction, and passion supplies the motivating energy for great achievements. When you have a purpose greater than yourself and a passion for your work, you seek out additional opportunities to exert yourself. Reaching a new milestone does not signal a stopping point but rather increases your conviction that you are on the right path. It spurs you to work even harder.

Whether you call it passion or ambition, you can feel an internal drive to sustain your effort, whether experiencing success or facing challenges. Your passions tie to your values, self-image, and personal history. You need sufficient self-awareness to recognize how your inner needs influence your values and choices so that you can engage your passions to serve a purpose beyond yourself. A sign of emotional maturity is when your ambition serves a social or organizational purpose, not just a narcissistic one.

Think of the differences between the top management of AHERF, who used the organization for their own ends and drove it into bankruptcy, and the senior team of the Mayo Clinic in Rochester, Minnesota, who live by the creed "The needs of the patient come first." Contrast Richard Scrushy, founder and former CEO of Health South, with Quint Studer, former CEO of Baptist Hospital in Pensacola, Florida, and now CEO of the Studer Group. Both are driven and ambitious, but Scrushy is under indictment for fraud while Studer is spreading a gospel of superior patient service with health systems around the country.

AHERF and Health South skyrocketed to regional and national prominence and crashed back to earth just as quickly. In contrast, Mayo not only endures but also prospers both as an organization and as a model of quality to be emulated by others. Baptist Hospital continues to win national recognition for patient and employee satisfaction even

several years after Studer's departure. In the case of both Mayo and Baptist, the organizations have purpose. The staff are aligned with that purpose and their values parallel those of the clinic or hospital. The leaders have sparked the passions of their staff so that there is no complacency or coasting but rather a continued drive to achieve the organizational mission. Success builds on success.

ASK YOURSELF

1. You cannot sustain maximum effort at *all* times. When do you coast?

2. How can you use momentum to help carry your organization forward without allowing success to make you complacent?

3. Can you identify your own equivalent of the Lehigh Gorge Rail Trail where your apparent success misled you? Where you were going downhill but did not realize it?

4. When you are tempted to coast and to "enjoy the fruits of your labors," what impels you to work instead of resting on your past successes?

5. What things drive you that are directed toward your own success and well-being, and what things

drive you that are other directed? You are likely to have some of both.

6. How do your personal aspirations align with the organization's mission? Where do they diverge? How can you create greater congruence for yourself and the people you lead?

7. Is there a shared vision in your organization that has engaged not only your commitment but also that of your colleagues? Does this vision lead to mutual support and foster widespread engagement in your organization?

LAST WORD

It is not enough for only you as a leader to have purpose and passion. For true success, a shared vision and commitment must be distributed widely throughout your entire organization. In the *Fifth Discipline*, Peter Senge (1990) introduces the concept of *learning organizations*. Such organizations reflect the natural tendency of humans to learn and to grow. In fact, they enable even more growth. This is in contrast to top-down organizations, where all direction comes from the top, or bureaucratic organizations, where rules and red tape stifle creativity and initiative. In learning organizations, leaders help everyone in the organization become a part of creating a strong and adaptive team. In a learning organization, you as leader are also teacher and steward, not the sole decision maker or the only or greatest authority. By building a shared vision and by communicating purpose and values, you help create an environment of energy and drive rather than one of self-satisfaction or complacency.

REFERENCES

Collins, J. 2001. *Good to Great: Why Some Companies Make the Leap...And Others Don't*. New York: HarperCollins.

Senge, P. M. 1990. *The Fifth Discipline*. New York: Currency.

CHAPTER 8

One-Dimensional Thinking Is Always Superficial

The First Law of Analysis

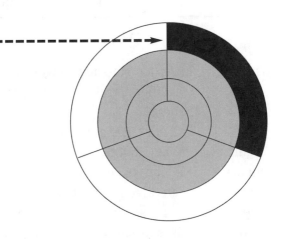

s it better to call patients *patients*? Or is it better to refer to them as *customers*? Many physicians cringe when they hear management use the term *customers*. For them, this is just one more marker of the decline and fall of American healthcare. Many administrators counter that this is a long overdue recognition of the rights of patients ▶

Figure 7. "Customer" Versus "Patient"

	Term of Reference	
	"Patient"	*"Customer"*
Advantages	• Traditional • Implies caring • Preferred by clinicians	• Implies service • Customer has rights and choices • Others besides patients are customers, including "internal customers"
Disadvantages	• May lock patients and physicians into traditional authority/ dependency roles • Ignores others being served	• Implies economic relationship as primary • Grates on ears of many patients and physicians • May lessen focus on patient as most important customer

and part of engaging patients as partners in their care.

I like to look at it in terms of a 2 × 2 table, as shown in Figure 7.

When you hear two people arguing over the distinction between patients and customers, you will often find that they talk past each other. The patient advocate will take a position equivalent to a diagonal line from upper left of the figure to lower right (the advantages of patient and disadvantages of customer). The customer advocate will argue just the opposite, from the upper right to the lower left (the advantages of customer and the disadvantages of patient).

Each takes a unidimensional point of view that oversimplifies the issue. Neither concedes the validity of the alternative perspective. However, often resolving differences such as this is as simple as creating a little chart like the one shown in Figure 7 to move a discussion from debate to dialog. If you lay out the options as done in the figure, you create the opportunity for both parties to consider merits and demerits

Figure 8. Humor in the Workplace

		Commitment	
		Yes	*No*
Humor	Yes	• Enthusiasm • Morale	• Silliness • Distraction
	No	• Serious • Determined	• Bureaucratic mindlessness

together. They may still choose differently. However, you will have helped them gain greater understanding of the options and the reasons why someone else may feel strongly about a position with which they disagree.

2 x 2 TABLES

You will find that looking at problems and opportunities from at least two directions adds far more insight than you get from a single perspective. Consider the charts that appear throughout this book. In each instance, I took a common problem or situation and tried to achieve a fresh look at it by creating a table with two columns and two rows. I intended each of these to be easy to understand and useful tools for you. Such 2 × 2 tables should help you think through issues and communicate better—both expressing your own ideas and opinions and hearing those of others.

Try this: next time you are in a discussion going nowhere, see if you can identify two different frames of reference or criteria that the speakers are using. Then see if you can create a 2 × 2 table that will consider both ideas at once. For example, I heard a couple of managers arguing over the appropriateness of humor in the workplace. One felt it was good for morale. The other contended that it could signal to patients or other staff a lack of commitment. I tried a 2 × 2 table to help them. I put commitment across the top and humor on the side and asked them to help me fill in the chart (Figure 8).

It took a minute or two to sketch in the descriptions. Not only did it help each of us see the issue from a couple of perspectives at once but it also got us working together. We became partners considering an issue, not opponents trying to score points in an argument. A 2 × 2 table is a simple tool that you can use on

Figure 9. Service Quality and Clinical Quality

		Clinical Quality	
		Low	High
Service Quality	High	• • • •	• • • •
	Low	• • • •	• • • •

the spot to help break out of one-dimensional thinking.

SERVICE AND QUALITY IN HEALTHCARE

When I first established a "customer" service program years ago, I faced conflicting views on the need and desirability of such training. Some staff were enthusiastic and adopted the term *customer* readily. Others resisted the notion saying that such an approach was superficial and demeaned the essential clinical priority of quality care. Once again, a 2 × 2 table helped me consider both

perspectives and display them in a way that brought insight to both factions. You could fill this table in yourself (Figure 9).

Put in each box what you think would be the experience, thoughts, feelings, or actions of people who received care in each of these four combinations of clinical and service quality. Try it now, before reading on.

What I found when I did this with numerous groups was a very high level of similarity of results regardless of the experience, training, profession, or sophistication of the group members. If they received both high service quality and high clinical quality, they said they would be delighted and would *probably tell others*. If, on the other hand, they received both low service quality and low clinical quality, they said they would be dismayed, would go elsewhere, and would *definitely tell others*. If they received high service quality but poor clinical quality, they might not recognize it at first but suggested they were likely to become disillusioned over time. If they received high clinical quality but poor service quality, they would recognize poor service right away. They would be irritated and frustrated but would stick with a high clinical quality provider—until they could find a more suitable alternative.

A chart and a discussion like this make it easier for people with different views to acknowledge and accept each other's insights. They can usually see how someone else might be using a different set of unspoken assumptions about what is most important. They can also recognize that things are not usually all bad or all good; there can also be mixed experiences. Administrators might be more inclined to look at the service dimension since that is what they understand best, and physicians and nurses might begin with the clinical quality dimension because it relates directly to their purpose and training. However, it should not be difficult for any of them to look at both dimensions simultaneously when given the opportunity with a chart like Figure 9.

About now, you might be agreeing that 2 × 2 charts are fine, but also thinking there are situations where 3 × 3 or 4 × 4 or even 2 × 2 × 2 charts would be better suited to the complexity of real life. You would be right, of course. There are many situations, for example, where looking at high, low, *and medium* adds a lot more insight than just high and low. You should feel free to add dimensions or levels as suits your situation or problem. However, I am constantly impressed by how much explanatory power can be achieved with the simplest table possible, the 2 × 2.

ASK YOURSELF

1. When you find yourself in a debate with a colleague where you seem to be talking past each other, are you able to get the discussion back on a constructive track? What has been successful for you?

2. As you have read through this book, which of the charts have

proven to be of the greatest use to you? Why?

3. Think of a work issue that is resisting resolution. Could a 2 × 2 chart help you clarify the conflicting points of view?

4. Often we are not consciously aware of the primary dimensions we use for judging people. What dimensions do you use? Are there one or two you use most?

5. Try constructing a 2 × 2 chart with skills or personality traits—for example, high and low analytical skills and high and low assertiveness. How would you describe people in each of the four boxes? Can you think of coworkers who fit those descriptions? How do they view each other?

6. In this chapter, I suggest that clinicians and managers are likely to differ on which dimension of care they consider the most important. Can you think of similar differences between management and staff or between first-line management and top management? How would you put those into a chart?

7. How could you use a 2 × 2 chart to simplify and clarify one of your current problems or priorities?

LAST WORD

What is the difference between simple and simplistic? A simple approach helps make things clearer by reducing complexity and getting to the essence of a situation. A simplistic approach, however, muddies issues by ignoring complexity and failing to get at root causes.

One-dimensional thinking is always superficial—and simplistic. A simple technique, such as a 2 × 2 table, on the other hand, can make problems or choices clearer without being overly analytical or abstract. Work and organizations can bog down when planning is simplistic or overly complex. The simple approach, as advocated in this chapter, is one of the best and easiest cures.

CHAPTER 9

If Everyone Is Doing It, Either It Is the Wrong Thing Or It Is Too Late

The Second Law of Strategy

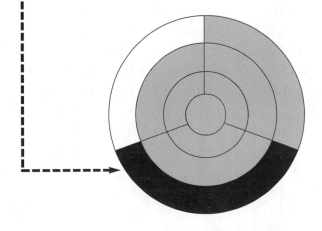

When your mother and father told you that just because *everyone* was doing something, it was not a good reason for you to do it too, they were right. In fact, they were not only teaching you a good lesson for life but they were also teaching you a good strategy lesson as well. It sometimes ▶

seems that healthcare executives are just like little kids. They spontaneously play follow the leader. And it gets them into trouble.

FOLLOW THE LEADER

Despite its massive size, healthcare is still just a cottage industry. The supplier side is dominated by giants. The payer side is coalescing into a smaller number of major players. But the provider side is made up of thousands of independent facilities and hundreds of thousands of independent practitioners. This means that there is a relatively low level of formal organization for an industry so large. Thus, instead of rules, policies, and coordinated strategies directing behavior, you will find fads, fashion, and tradition influencing the actions of many institutions and individuals.

Have you ever watched a large flock of birds flying together? They dip, turn, and rise as a group. To an observer on the ground, they appear more like a single unit than like multiple individuals. Some simple rules arising from species' instinct lead each bird to adjust its own flight patterns to keep in sync with its neighbors. I wonder if an observer

from another planet watching healthcare leaders would conclude that we function with a similar species' instinct.

Think of how hospitals and health systems handled the emergence of managed care. As usual, the leading-edge areas of the country, like California, encountered the challenge first. Among the hospitals and physicians there, a few reacted quickly and embraced the new payment model. Almost overnight, they became the role models for their peers around the country. Consultants jumped on the bandwagon and preached the gospel of capitation across the country. Providers scrambled to get on board. No one wanted to be left behind. No one wanted to miss the opportunity to reap the same type of financial windfall claimed by the West Coast innovators. However, global capitation never became a dominant payment form, and few fortunes were made because of it.

Thus, healthcare played follow the leader. Managers and executives thought they were being strategic, but they were imitating, not innovating. When you travel in a group, you arrive at the same destination and at the same time as everyone else. If you move a little faster or push a little harder, you may get there earlier, but you will not be alone for long. The essence of strategy is not sameness but differentiation.

DIFFERENTIATION

In *Competing for the Future*, Hamel and Prahalad (1994) propose that the most successful organizations are the ones that redefine their industries. For example, you might think of the way that Johns Hopkins revolutionized medical education in the late nineteenth century by combining basic science education and intensive clinical experience. Leading organizations seek to create something new, not to fit into the world as it currently exists. Hamel and Prahalad (1994, 22) argue that it is not enough to be better or faster; you also need to be different.

> Competition for the future is competition to create and dominate emerging opportunities—to stake out new competitive space. Creating the future is more challenging than playing catch-up, in that you have to create your own road map. The goal is not simply to benchmark a competitor's products and processes and imitate its methods, but to develop an independent point of view about tomorrow's opportunities and how to exploit them.

As you look at your own organization or your own division or department, you want to ask how you are *different* from everyone else. This is likely to be a very uncomfortable question. It goes against so much formal education and on-the-job training in healthcare.

For example, I once reported to a very talented CEO who was forward looking and an excellent planner. However, one of his standard questions in response to a new proposal was to ask who else was doing it in healthcare. If there were not already successful hospital exemplars, he would be very skeptical about the merits of the idea. I have been surprised when I have heard myself ask the same question, despite my belief in the advantages of being different. It is almost like hearing myself repeat to my children the same things my parents said to me.

You are likely to find that your organization, too, works to keep things the same and against being different. The structure and culture of healthcare in our country reinforce that pattern. It is tough risking to be different when resources and margins are so thin. Keeping your organization the same creates a "me too" approach to strategy. What is said about sled dogs is true for organizations as well: "If you're not the lead dog, the view never changes."

BUY LOW/SELL HIGH

Is there *anyone* who does not know this fundamental rule of economics? Why is it violated so often? The principle is simple; the execution is difficult. You can see the problem in any boom and bust cycle on Wall Street. There are stock analysts now who believe one of the surest signs of the end of a boom and beginning of a bust is when the media report that a boom is in full swing. The great advantage goes to the early movers or early adopters. By contrast, latecomers pay too much and get too little.

If you are not a leader, you may still need to jump on the bandwagon, but only to "stay in the game," not to gain a strategic advantage over your competition. When the Internet was first showing signs of commercial applicability, our organization decided to experiment by providing access to a small pilot group of staff. Management did not want to overinvest in a new technology or risk distractions at work. Over the course of the next decade, Internet access changed from being an exotic option to being built into every desktop PC.

You will get no strategic advantage now by merely being on the net. If you want to gain an advantage, you will need to identify different uses of being on the net, ways that would reshape how you work. That is the strategic equivalent of "buying low."

· ASK YOURSELF

1. What are some healthcare industry trends or ideas that your organization latched onto in seeking a financial or competitive edge, only to find the rewards much slimmer than expected?
2. Has your organization achieved any of the benefits of differentiation? How did you accomplish that?
3. Does your stated organizational strategy highlight ways in which

you can become a market or industry leader by doing things differently than others?

4. How do you take advantage of best practices and benchmarking without merely imitating market leaders?

5. What are some of the ways that you or other leaders in your organization encourage staff to play it safe by being the same rather than taking the risk of being different?

6. Have you discovered opportunities or trends early enough in the cycle to gain a competitive advantage? Did you act on that insight, or hesitate? Why?

7. Given your skills or the strengths and assets of your organization, are there areas where you can deliver greater value to your patients or customers in ways that would be difficult for others to copy?

LAST WORD

When you strip away all of the frills and complexities, the essence of strategy is for you to discover ways to add *value* for your patients or customers better than your competitors can. Beginning with roughly the same resources as your competition, what can you do differently that would induce patients to choose your organization over theirs? In marketing terms, what is your value proposition?

If everyone else is doing it, either it is the wrong thing, or it is too late in terms of creating competitive advantage. It may have become a cost of doing business, a must-have. It is not, however, a strategic action. Your strategy is your plan for creating value for your patients or customers in ways that set you apart from your competition. You establish the rules of the game by getting there first.

REFERENCE

Hamel, G., and C. K. Prahalad. 1994. *Competing for the Future*. Boston: Harvard Business School Press.

CHAPTER 10

Stop and Smell the Roses

The First Law of Executive Stamina

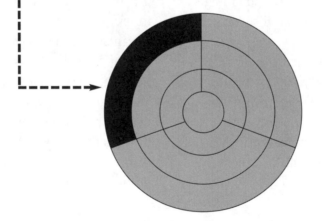

You are watching a NASCAR race. With 20 laps to go, one of the lead cars brushes the wall, spins, flips, bounces, and rolls to the edge of the infield. The caution flag comes out, a crew sprints onto the grass to spray fire retardant on the car, and the driver climbs from the window and waves to show he or she is unhurt. Most of the leaders pull into pit row on the next lap to gas up and change tires while the race is under the yellow flag. A few follow a different ▶

strategy. They skip the pits and pass the cars that are refueling, calculating that they have enough gas to finish the race. When the wreck is cleared and the starter waves the green flag, the drivers push their vehicles hard to defend their positions or to overtake the cars ahead. Those with fresh tires pick up valuable seconds. You wonder if the drivers who did not pit will be able to hang on. Will they run out of gas even when the end is within sight? You will not know the answers until each driver actually passes the finish line.

What about you? Ever wonder if you can hang on? Wonder if you will run out of gas before you are done?

PACING

The secret is in pacing—building in renewal and refreshment. As a healthcare leader, you need your own personal pit row. You need to know when to slow down, to stop, to recover. And you need to know how much is in your tank—how hard and how fast you can push for how long.

"We're wired up but we're melting down." So say performance psychologist Jim Loehr and coauthor Tony Schwartz in *The Power of Full Engagement* (Loehr and Schwartz 2003, 3). For more than 30 years, they have worked with professional athletes to help them manage their energy better. As time passed, they began to consult with business people as well. What they found there surprised them, even if it does not surprise you: "The performance demands that most people face in their everyday work environments dwarf those of any professional athletes we have ever trained" (Loehr and Schwartz 2003, 8). To meet those demands takes energy—lots of it— physical, emotional, mental, and spiritual.

According to Loehr and Schwartz, professional athletes who perform at peak levels achieve those results by alternating periods of intense effort with periods of recovery. They develop habits or rituals that relieve stress and restore focus.

If you are a tennis fan, you may recall the routine that Ivan Lendl went through before *every* serve. He "wiped his brow with his wristband, knocked the head of his racquet against each of his heels, took sawdust from his pocket, bounced the ball four times..." (Loehr and Schwartz 2003, 172). He brought down his pulse rate and respiration and recovered energy and focus. Jack Nicklaus did likewise in golf. He developed a routine for alternating concentration and relaxation as he prepared to hit from the tee and then as he walked down the fairway for his next shot (Loehr and Schwartz 2003, 33–34).

Loehr and Schwartz say that you and I need to do the same if we too want to maximize our performance. You may feel that managing a clinic or hospital is like running a marathon, but they suggest that you are better off treating it as a series of sprints rather than as one long, steady effort—that is, if you want to perform like top athletes do. You need to build periods of renewal and recovery into your workday and workweek. If you are running flat out all the time, you begin to lose speed and effectiveness despite your level of perceived effort. Without proper pacing, work becomes a rat race and a grind. If you are feeling flat, dispirited, or exhausted, that is a good clue that you have not established effective energy recovery rituals.

Creating a Sustainable Pace for Others

What do you do if your team shows the same signs of burnout? You, as leader, have a responsibility to help manage their energy levels as well as

your own. In *Best Laid Plans*, Rouse (1994) uses hiking stories as a metaphor for managing others. Imagine that you are hiking up a long, steep mountain trail. After a while, all you see is the back of the person in front of you. After a bit more, all you see are your own feet, as your head is down from the effort and you watch yourself take one step after another. Such effort can become grim and unpleasant after an hour or two. You start to question why you are on the mountain in the first place. A good hike leader, therefore, will plan a route that includes interesting places to take a break, to eat, to rest, or to look around. Perhaps the leader will stop in a wildflower meadow or on a rock ledge that provides a panorama of the valley so you can look back and see the progress you have made. When you put on your pack to continue up the trail after a break like that, you will do so with more energy, a lighter step, and perhaps a smile.

The good hike leader creates a rhythm or pace that alternates effort with refreshment. When you are leading others in healthcare, you need to do likewise. You do not want your department managers figuratively walking around with their heads down watching their own feet, just trying to make it through the next week. You want to plan work so that there are breaks, times and places to feel satisfaction, and opportunities to celebrate what has been accomplished so far, even if the whole job is still incomplete. Your goal, like the hike leader, is to help your staff perform at their best. You want to make it possible for them to go further than they thought themselves capable, but not by driving them relentlessly. Instead, you plan a route that allows you and them to stop every so often and smell the roses. You enjoy the journey more, they enjoy it more, and you can get a lot more done without running out of gas.

WORK/LIFE BALANCE

Even when you figure out how to perform at peak levels at work, however, you may still find yourself unable to achieve a satisfactory balance between work and home responsibilities. This challenge has defeated many executives. Many healthcare leadership positions are 24/7. The demands and the stimulation of work may push your personal plans aside. You may find yourself referring to family and home activities as "obligations," not as

opportunities or pleasures. You feel pulled and tugged. You become distracted both at work and at home. The next step is defensiveness, and then resentment. Surely a negative spiral, if ever there was one.

Perhaps more than any other topic in this entire book, the issue of work/life balance depends on your frame of mind. It demands self-awareness. It requires that you know in your gut—not just in your head— what is important to you. In Chapter 1, I describe my observations as a psychologist that human beings have a significant capacity for self-deception. Look again on page 7 at the list of reasons why you may not always do the things you know you should do. Rereading them in the context of this chapter should make it clear that those are also reasons why your words and your actions may not match when it comes to work/life balance.

Work/Life Synergy

But wait! There is good news. Try reframing the concept of work/life balance. Think about it instead as *work/life synergy*. Balance is not a bad word, but it seems to imply, in this instance, work/life *trade-off*. Balance conjures up a picture of making compromises between work demands and home demands—not fully meeting the needs of either. The word *synergy*, however, suggests that the two can work together to supplement and enhance each other. If the preceding section on pacing is correct, work life and home life can serve as places of renewal and refreshment for each other. An active personal life should make you fitter for work. A satisfying work life should carry over to home. This does not happen automatically, however. You need to be self-aware and recognize how you are managing your physical, emotional, mental, and spiritual energy, deliberately seeking refreshment and renewal in each sphere.

A nurse said to me recently that she feels blessed because she looks forward to coming into work each morning and looks forward to going home each evening. I think she got that exactly right.

ASK YOURSELF

1. When the pressure is on, do you ever wonder if you can hang on? Do you wonder if you will run out of gas before you are done? When? What kinds of situations make you feel that way?

2. What signals tell you that you need to take a break? How do you respond to those signals?

3. Professional athletes, like Lendl and Nicklaus, have recovery rituals to enable them to regain control, energy, and focus. What about you?

4. A great way to renew energy is through fun and laughter. As a leader, how do you encourage fun and laughter at work?

5. What kinds of breaks can you build in at work that will help your team appreciate their progress and become reenergized for the challenges ahead?

6. What things do you do outside of work that give you the greatest satisfaction? In what ways do they help you be a better leader at work?

7. What things do you do simply because you enjoy them?

LAST WORD

One of the major factors that relates to maintaining enthusiasm at work is the ability to recognize and take opportunities for *leisure* outside of work. When I consulted with senior executives across a broad range of industries, in healthcare and otherwise, I noted that many of the most successful seemed to have hobbies that engaged their energy and attention, and in some cases, passion. I wondered how they could achieve such positive results in contrast to many of their less successful colleagues, who worked longer hours. I concluded that they approached work with greater clarity, more vigor, and more frequent bursts of creativity or insight.

I also saw that they frequently made "connections" through their leisure activities that nourished their work. Sometimes these were intuitive leaps, sometimes life lessons, and occasionally interesting people. Such connections seemed to come most frequently when they were not seeking them, however.

Leisure is like that. It allows you access to parts of your mind and personality that cannot be opened by a direct or logical approach. Even if it involves vigorous physical or mental activity, leisure can leave you feeling physically and psychologically renewed, more ready and more able to take on challenges. Stopping and smelling the roses can be an effective antidote to burnout and a key to success and longevity in your work.

REFERENCES

Loehr, J., and T. Schwartz. 2003. *The Power of Full Engagement*. New York: Free Press.

Rouse, W. B. 1994. *Best Laid Plans*. Upper Saddle River, NJ: Prentice Hall.

Conclusion

My aim in this book is to share some stories and insights to help you to achieve more and to experience more satisfaction as a healthcare leader and as a manager. You know, and I know, that learning to be a leader is a lifelong process. I hope that this book can be a companion for you, like a coach, to help you sharpen your self-awareness and refine your skills. Finishing the book, therefore, is not an ending but rather the beginning of the next phase of your personal learning process.

THE TEN LAWS REVISITED

1. Do the Right Thing (the First Law of Leadership)—Knowing right and doing right are not the same things. Leadership takes both thought and courage.
2. There Is No *Right* Way (the First Law of Management)—As a manager, you need to anticipate and understand side effects and be prepared to deal with them.
3. Leadership Is an Action, Not a Title (the Second Law of Leadership)—You gain legitimacy by what you do, not by the title on your name badge. If you want to make an impact as a leader, your actions must speak as loudly as your words.
4. Ready…Aim…Fire (the First Law of Strategy)—When you combine vision and action, you can achieve the greatest results and derive the most satisfaction from your work.
5. If You Can't Measure It, You Can't Improve It (the First Law of Measurement)—How can you get better if you cannot measure results, identify mistakes, make adjustments, and measure again? Not measuring results is like playing a game without knowing how score is kept.
6. If You and I Are Always in Agreement, One of Us Is Not

Necessary (the First Law of Diversity)—Too much agreement can be as harmful to effective teamwork as too little. If you watch the work of a good team, you will see different members call on their strengths to contribute to team process.

7. If You Are Coasting, You Are Going Downhill (the First Law of Competitive Physics)—In healthcare, you need to stay on top of your game, or you will lose ground quickly, even if it is not obvious at first. For true success, you must create a compelling vision for yourself and your followers that will spur you to overcome all obstacles.

8. One-Dimensional Thinking Is Always Superficial (the First Law of Analysis)—A 2×2 table is a simple tool you can use to organize different perspectives and help make problems or choices clearer.

9. If Everyone Is Doing It, Either It Is the Wrong Thing, Or It Is Too Late (the Second Law of Strategy)—Healthcare managers play follow the leader, but when you travel in a group, you arrive at the same destination at the same time as everyone else. The essence of strategy is not sameness but differentiation. Buy low and sell high.

10. Stop and Smell the Roses (the First Law of Executive Stamina)—Jobs at all levels in healthcare have high burnout potential. You need to know when to slow down, to stop, to recover—and how to help those who report to you to do likewise. Those who perform at peak levels alternate periods of intense effort with periods of recovery, and they enjoy the journey more.

ASK YOURSELF

1. What have you learned about yourself that will help you be a better leader of others?

2. Have you developed a personal mission statement? Have you shared it with anyone?

3. What tools can you use to help others achieve more and get greater satisfaction from their work?

4. What actions can you take to make your department or your organization a high-performance team?

5. Since our short-term memories are so limited and old habits are so hard to break, what practices

will you institute so that you will not forget the ideas or insights you gained while reading this book?

LAST WORD

One More Law

There is another law that many managers follow. In fact, many have told me that it is the centerpiece of their management philosophy. That law is the golden rule: Treat others as *you* would like to be treated.

As this book is closing, I would like to offer one more law, the successor to the golden rule. It goes one step further. I like to call this variation the *platinum* rule. The platinum rule directs you to *treat others as they would like to be treated*. The golden rule begins with fairness and equity. The platinum rule adds empathy. Together, they are a powerful combination.

Suggested Reading List

Collins, J. 2001. *Good to Great: Why Some Companies Make the Leap...And Others Don't*. New York: HarperCollins.

Covey, S. R. 1990. *The Seven Habits of Highly Effective People: Restoring the Character Ethic*. New York: Simon & Schuster.

Covey, S. R., A. R. Merrill, and R. R. Merrill. 1995. *First Things First: To Live, to Love, to Learn, to Leave a Legacy*. New York: Simon & Schuster.

George, B. 2003. *Authentic Leadership: Rediscovering the Secrets to Creating Lasting Value*. San Francisco: Jossey-Bass.

Hamel, G., and C. K. Prahalad. 1994. *Competing for the Future*. Boston: Harvard Business School Press.

Hammer, M., and J. Champy. 1993. *Reengineering the Corporation: A Manifesto for Business Revolution*. New York: Harper Business.

Janis, I. 1982. *Groupthink: Psychological Studies of Policy Decisions and Fiascoes*, 2nd ed. Boston: Houghton Mifflin.

Kaplan, R., and D. Norton. 1996. *The Balanced Scorecard: Translating Strategy into Action*. Boston: Harvard Business School Publishing.

Lakein, A. 1974. *How to Get Control of Your Time and Your Life*. New York: Penguin.

Lewis, M. 2003. *Moneyball: The Art of Winning an Unfair Game*. New York: W.W. Norton.

Loehr, J., and T. Schwartz. 2003. *The Power of Full Engagement*. New York: Free Press.

Rohrer, Hibler & Replogle, Inc. 1981. *The Managerial Challenge: A Psychological Approach to the Changing World of Management*. New York: The New American Library.

Rouse, W. B. 1994. *Best Laid Plans*. Upper Saddle River, NJ: Prentice Hall.

Senge, P. M. 1990. *The Fifth Discipline*. New York: Currency.

Useem, M. 2001. *Leading Up: How to Lead Your Boss So You Both Win*. New York: Crown Business.

Acknowledgments

This book grew out of a lifetime of lessons learned from friends, family, and colleagues. I couldn't possibly thank them all by name, but I hope my day-to-day actions convey my acknowledgment of what they have taught me. Alan Zuckerman provided the initial encouragement for me to put these ideas into book form and suggested Health Administration Press to publish it. A great recommendation—I have found the editors and staff to be a delight to work with. I called on many of my friends to read and comment on early drafts and am grateful for their assistance. I imposed, perhaps most of all, on two of the busiest people I know, Lynne Cunningham and Dan Sisto, and they came through with insightful advice, as I anticipated they would. My two daughters, Katie McGinn and Kerry Luse, provided the most detailed reviews of early chapters and greatly influenced the style and substance of the manuscript. My wife, Marilyn McGinn, provided space, support, and encouragement throughout, as is her way. I dedicate this book to my father, Vincent McGinn, a role model of ethical behavior and personal responsibility, and to the memory of my mother, Alice McGinn, who challenged me to build on the insights of others but in the end to think for myself.

About the Author

Peter McGinn, Ph.D., is president and CEO of United Health Services, a not-for-profit health system serving the Southern Tier region of New York. He is also chair-elect of the Healthcare Association of New York State.

Dr. McGinn earned his Ph.D. in psychology from the Johns Hopkins University. In his 30-year career, he has been a school psychologist, a U.S. Senate staff member, a clinical psychologist, a management consultant, and a healthcare senior manager. Early in his training, he concluded that two common life experiences, *going to school* and *going to work*, were creating more unhappy and dysfunctional people than he could treat in a lifetime of therapy. That conclusion was the impetus for seeking nontraditional routes to make a difference as a psychologist. His professional career has focused on making work places both more effective and more humane creating environments where people can use their energies and talents productively for their own well-being and for the benefit of their organizations. This philosophy is reflected in the vision of United Health Services: "To be a great place to work, and a great place to receive care."

Also by Health Administration Press

Do your part to build a culture that promotes patient safety and quality

Leading a Patient-Safe Organization
Matthew J. Lambert III, M.D., FACHE

If you are like most executives, you have delegated the details of clinical quality to the medical staff. But with increasing demands from the public, the media, insurers, and the federal government, patient safety is becoming an issue on which healthcare executives must focus. Do you understand your critical role in developing a patient-safe organization?

This book discusses what you need to know about medical error and about fostering a culture of safety. It provides straightforward information on such topics as:

- National quality improvement programs, which can guide you in responding to what is happening in the field
- The different types of errors encountered in healthcare and their common causes
- The physician versus executive perspective on error reduction and ways that you can find common ground
- The strategies for developing a culture that encourages open discussion of errors

For more information on this text, or to place an order, please visit:
www.ache.org/pubs/lambert.cfm